GREAT
OCEAN LINERS

The P&O liner Rome, *launched in 1881. Exceeding 5000 tons, she was designed for the Australian service.*

GREAT OCEAN LINERS

THE HEYDAY OF LUXURY TRAVEL

IAN DEAR

B. T. Batsford Ltd, London

© Ian Dear 1991
First published 1991

ISBN 0 7134 6026 1

Typeset by Tradespools Ltd, Frome, Somerset,
and printed in Great Britain by
The Bath Press, Bath
for the publishers
B.T. Batsford Ltd
4 Fitzhardinge Street
London W1H 0AH

CONTENTS

The promenade deck of the Great Britain. *On either side are the passengers' cabins.*

ACKNOWLEDGEMENTS

Thanks are due to the following for their help and permission to use the photographs in this book: Alfred Craske, London (49); Foto HAPAG-Lloyd AG, Hamburg (19–21, 24, 25, 27–29, 32–40, 50–58, 92, 102, 103, 107–109); French Line, Le Havre (59–61, 75, 76, 81–87); Lawrence Dunn (111a–d); Photography Department, Liverpool Museum (22); Photo Caption, Photogrpahic Library Group, Public Relations Department, P&O (frontispiece, 6—13, 17, 18, 26, 48, 65–74, 77, 78, 95, 96, 110); The Picture Company, Bristol (5); The University Archives, University of Liverpool (3, 4, 15, 16, 30, 31, 42, 44–46, 62–64, 79, 80, 88–91, 93, 94, 97–101, 104–106).

2 *The dining saloon of the* Great Britain.

INTRODUCTION

EARLY LINERS AND PASSENGER TRAVEL

The evolution of the ocean liner—which can be defined as a power-driven passenger ship on a regular, scheduled ocean route—began with the introduction of the marine steam engine during the early part of the nineteenth century. The first ship equipped with an engine to cross an ocean was a small coastal paddle-steamer called the *Savannah* which crossed from Savannah to Liverpool in May 1819. Her small single-cylinder engine had been put in as an afterthought and the captain soon found that using wind and steam power together did not work. One paddle dug deep into the water when she heeled under sail while the other beat on nothing but air, making her go round in circles. As a result, only 85 hours of the 27-day passage were spent under power.

In the years following *Savannah*'s historic voyage steamships sailed the other oceans of the world, though they all relied more on their sails than on their engines. In 1823 the Indian government offered a large cash sum for anyone who could establish a regular, 70-day mail service between England and Calcutta before the end of 1826. No one succeeded but soon the lucrative business of delivering the mails across the oceans on a regular basis became the spur for founding the great steamship lines which were to dominate the world of transport from Victorian times up to, and even beyond, the Second World War.

Full Steam Power

It was not until 1833, however, that a big enough vessel was built to carry sufficient fuel to cross the Atlantic under steam power alone. The *Cape Breton* was the first to cross,

from Britain to Nova Scotia, and a fortnight later the 800-ton *Royal William* crossed from Nova Scotia to Cowes on the Isle of Wight in 21 days with eight passengers aboard. Each day salt had to be cleared from her boilers, a process which took four hours, but this was the only time she used her sails. A Nova Scotian named Samuel Cunard had a financial interest in the *Royal William*, and her passage—as well as those that followed immediately after her—inspired him to found in 1840 the great steamship line which still carries his name today.

The first steamers to compete in establishing a regular mail and passenger route across the North Atlantic were the 208-ft coastal steamer *Sirius* and the 236-ft paddle steamer *Great Western*, designed by the famous engineer Isambard Kingdom Brunel for the Great Western Steamship Company. The *Great Western*'s great length compared with other vessels of her day was a result of Brunel's theory that the longer the hull the more economically it could be driven through the water. He proved to be correct and his theory can be said to be the basis for the construction of the great ocean liners that were to follow over the next century or more. Altogether the *Great Western* made 64 crossings of the North Atlantic, an achievement which resulted in her being called the first true transatlantic liner.

A rival of Brunel's ambition to start a regular service across the Atlantic was an American called Junius Smith. He, too, was building a steamship that was intended to dominate the North Atlantic run. But when he found that his new ship would not be ready to compete against the *Great Western* he chartered the *Sirius*. She was fitted with surface condensers, which meant no delays while the salt was cleaned from her boilers. Brunel's design sailed late so that the smaller ship had three days' lead. Nevertheless, the voyage proved to be a triumph for Brunel as the *Great Western* arrived less than four hours behind her rival. Significantly, the *Sirius* ran out of fuel during the crossing and was forced to burn spare spars; the *Great Western*, on the other hand, still had more than 40 tons of coal in her bunkers when she berthed.

Iron Hull and Screw Propeller

The success of the *Great Western* and other wooden paddle-steamers encouraged the Great Western Steamship Company to commission Brunel to design a second transatlantic passenger ship. This was the 322-ft *Great Britain*, by far the largest ship built in her time, launched in 1843. She was the first iron-built passenger ship, and also the first screw propeller ship to cross the Atlantic. She made her maiden voyage in July 1845 with 60 passengers and more than 600 tons of cargo aboard. She ran aground the following year on the Irish coast and the cost of salvaging her bankrupted her owners, who were

forced to sell her. In August 1852 she started the first of 32 successful round voyages to Australia, mostly under sail. After lying abandoned in the Falkland Islands for decades she has now been restored and is on view in Bristol, her original home port, a fascinating reminder of the earliest form of passenger liner.

Brunel then designed the *Great Eastern* for the Eastern Navigation Company. She was launched in 1858, but was ahead of her time and was a commercial failure. She was a massive vessel 692 feet long with a beam of nearly 83 feet, and unique in that she was driven by both paddle and screw propeller, as well as having six masts that carried 6500 sq ft of canvas. She could carry 800 first-class, 2000 second-class, and 1200 third-class passengers, and was the first ship on which there was sufficient space for passengers to pass the time with deck games. On her maiden voyage there was a marathon and someone even set up some ninepins. From this modest beginning sprang a variety of entertainments, organized first by the passengers themselves, but in modern times by shipping companies anxious to keep their customers occupied and happy.

EARLY SHIPPING LINES

While Brunel was active in designing the forerunners to the great liners of the twentieth century, the companies that were to run them came into being. The Peninsular Steam Navigation Company was started by two Londoners, Arther Anderson and Brodie Willcox, who chartered a steamer in 1836 for trading between Spain and Britain. The following year they won an Admiralty contract to deliver mail between Lisbon, Cadiz, and Gibraltar. In 1840 they won another contract to take the mails to Alexandria, whence it was sent overland to Suez and then on to India by sea. In 1845 the mail service was extended to Singapore and Hong Kong, and in the early 1850s, to Australia.

The P&O Line

During these years the 'Line', now called the Peninsular and Oriental Steam Navigation Company—or P&O for short—rapidly made a name for itself for the quality of its service. Its officers were of the highest standard—their dress and demeanour were hard to distinguish from those of an officer in the Royal Navy—as were the ships and their crews, and the passengers always seemed to receive value for their money. Both food and drink were at first included in the price of a ticket. The food was plentiful and though mainly English in origin the Indian curries that were also served became renowned. Fresh meat was mainly carried live and the company's practice was to have sufficient livestock aboard for the voyage from Southampton to Alexandria. The ship from Suez was then

provisioned by a farm which the company maintained there.

In the first decades of the 'Line' there was plenty of liquor, too, starting with claret for breakfast and ending with a nightcap of brandy or gin, or both, while champagne flowed whenever approaching or leaving harbour. By the 1880s, however, all passengers had to pay for their drink.

The accommodation of the early steamers was more or less as it had been in sailing ships, and was extremely sparse. Even first-class cabins held as many as four bunks, and there was only one saloon—situated aft—in which to eat, drink, read, play games, or chat. The passengers ate at a long central table with benches either side and the ship was lit at night by candlelight. Because of the ever-present danger of fire all lights had to be extinguished by 10:30 pm or 11:00 pm, and this was strictly enforced.

P&O did not cater for emigrants in these early days—and did not do so until it took over the Blue Anchor Line in 1910—so its ships were divided between first-class passengers (the gentry, senior Indian civil servants, army officers) and their servants, who went second class, as did missionaries and some clergymen who were too poor to travel first class. The days were spent in writing diaries and playing games, while the evenings were passed with concerts, sing-songs and dances, all enlivened, no doubt, by the young ladies, known as the 'fishing fleet', who were on their way to India in the hope of finding husbands among the British Raj.

Because of the length of the voyage and the type of passenger it carried, Victoran protocol ruled the P&O to a greater extent than it did other lines. It really mattered who sat at the Captain's table and who had the best cabin. Port Out, Starboard Home meant you had a cabin away from the sun on both the outward and homeward voyage and indicated you were someone of influence and importance. Hence the word 'posh'—though no one knows for sure that this is the correct origin of the word.

Until the opening of the Suez Canal in November 1869 part of a passenger's journey had to be overland to make a connection with a ship in the Red Sea, and in its early days the P&O did much to lessen the hardships of this part of the voyage. Eventually a railway was built from Cairo, which further improved the speed and comfort when passengers travelled overland. However, it was often still far from pleasant, as one of the passengers who went P&O to India in 1858 noted in his diary:

We left Cairo early in the morning by train but, after an hour's journey, the railway suddenly left off in the middle of the desert. Our baggage was put on camels led by Abraham, Isaac and Jacob living in the flesh, and the passengers were closely packed into small green omnibuses on two wheels drawn by mules, six of us in each. There

was a long procession of them and they plunged and jolted most uncomfortably. We reached dirty Suez as the sun was setting and after a wretched fly-haunted meal in the bare caravanserai of an hotel, went on board the 'Bengal', a large roomy old tub of a vessel.

It might be thought that the opening of the Canal would have been a boon to the P&O, but initially the reverse was true. Its ships were unsuitable for the new waterway, which made the buildings and equipment used for the overland route redundant. Rivals quickly built ships that could use the new route and were capable of carrying cargo at far better rates than the P&O.

Luckily, with the introduction of the much more economical compound engine, the company had to rebuild its fleet anyway, and the decision was made to continue with high-quality steamers that provided a first-class service. This proved to be a wise investment, and by 1884 the fleet was back to 50 ships, each about twice the average size of those owned 15 years previously. However, they remained old-fashioned in several ways: there was no proper room where the men could smoke, candles continued to be used so that the 'lights out' rule still had to be enforced, and the first-class saloon remained situated, uncomfortably, over the propeller.

There must have been adverse comments made by passengers who had travelled on the much more comfortable transatlantic liners of the period, for in 1878 P&O launched the 4000-ton *Kaisar-i-Hind* which was equipped with many new luxuries. She was a great success and proved to the Line's directors that passengers travelling to the East were as fond of their comforts as those crossing the Atlantic, and from then on the standards of every P&O ship launched rose steadily.

During the Victorian days of the British Empire the P&O always had a glamour all its own, quite different in style and outlook to the rakish transatlantic run, where from the beginning the battle to lure passengers on to the latest, ritziest liner was always fierce and unremitting.

The Cunard Line

The roots of this competition go back to a date in February 1839 when Samuel Cunard submitted a tender to procure the lucrative mail contract between England and Halifax, and between Halifax and America. The contract stipulated that the vessels used had to be steamships of not less than 330 hp, and they were to be run on a monthly schedule from one of five ports: Liverpool, Bristol, Plymouth, Falmouth or Southampton. The first contract was signed on 4 May 1839, but others stipulating the size of the ships and the

amount of payments to be made continued to be negotiated throughout that year and on into 1840. Once concluded, Cunard, and his partners David and Charles MacIver and George and James Burns, founded the British and North American Royal Mail Steam Packet Company and ordered four ships: *Britannia*, *Columbia*, *Acadia*, and *Caledonia*. Each was about 1150 tons, was powered by 420 hp Napier engines, and could accommodate approximately 100 passengers. But unlike some other passenger ships of the day— the *Great Western* for example—the ships were sparsely fitted out, with Samuel Cunard directing his builders thus: 'I want a plain and comfortable boat, not the least unnecessary expense for show,' he stated. 'I prefer plain work in the cabin and it will save a large amount in the cost.' His instructions to his captains show where his priorities lay: 'Your ship is loaded, take her; speed is nothing, follow your own road, deliver her safe, bring her back safe—safety is all that is required.'

The first of these vessels, *Britannia*, made her maiden voyage in July 1840. Two years later the novelist Charles Dickens sailed in her to America to undertake a lecture tour. He does not seem to have been left with a good impression:

> Before descending into the bowels of the ship, we had passed from the deck into a long and narrow apartment, not unlike a gigantic hearse with windows in the sides: having at the upper end a melancholy stove, at which three or four chilly stewards were warming their hands; while on either side, extending down its whole dreary length, was a long, long, table; over which a rack, fixed to the low roof, and stuck full of drinking-glasses and cruet-stands, hinted dismally at rolling seas and heavy weather.

His foreboding was fully justified for it was a rough crossing and he and his wife, and his wife's maid, were all thoroughly seasick. To make matters worse the boat creaked badly, the cook got drunk, the saloon fire was rarely alight, and the whole nightmare lasted for 18 days. Dickens returned by sailing packet.

Though always under commercial pressure, Samuel Cunard was slow to adapt to new technology, preferring to leave it to others to experiment with innovations like iron hulls, the screw propeller, the compound engine, and later the triple expansion engine, all of which made passenger ships faster, more reliable, and, crucially, more economical. This policy had its rewards, for not only was Samuel Cunard spared the costs of development, but his ships attained an enviable record for reliability and safety, and it was on this foundation that the company eventually built its reputation as the world's premier passenger shipping line. During its first 35 years of operations—when travelling by sea was a high-risk undertaking, and when both the White Star Line and the Inman Line lost ships and passengers—no life was lost aboard a Cunarder, a truly outstanding record.

Though conservatively built, Samuel Cunard's wooden-hulled paddle steamships doubled in size between 1840 and 1852 and the power of their enginers quadrupled. After the latter date he began to build iron-hulled steamships, and later screw-driven ones, both these innovations having already been successfully exploited by the Inman line.

Samuel Cunard died in 1865, but the family interest in the company was maintained by his two sons, Edward and William. Edward died in 1869 and his shares were taken over by his brother. In 1878 the company's name was changed to The Cunard Steam Ship Co. Ltd. and, with profits boosted by entry in 1860 into the business of carrying emigrants, its fleet had grown to 28 ships by 1880, all but nine of which were operating across the Atlantic.

The Inman and American Lines

William Inman was a true innovator and his *City of Glasgow*, which went into service in 1852, could be regarded as the turning point not only in the design of liners but in the development of the passenger trade, for she was able to prove that, on the North Atlantic run at least, it was possible to carry passengers without having to have a mail contract to make such a service profitable. She was able to do so because she was the first regular transaltantic liner to carry emigrants, a form of trade which became increasingly important as the century progressed. She was, incidentally, also the first liner to be fitted with a spar deck, which covered part of her main deck. 'A magnificent promenade in fine weather,' eulogized a Glasgow newspaper of the time, 'and in foul weather the main deck afforded ample space for recreation, perfectly lighted and ventilated and protected from rain or spray.' Another Inman ship, the *City of Berlin*, was the first to be fitted, in 1879, with electric lighting, and this became standard aboard the bigger passenger liners during the following decade, way ahead of its use in public places ashore.

In the early 1890s the Inman Line was bought by the International Navigation Company of Philadelphia, which then renamed itself the American Line. With two new ships, the *St Louis* and the *St Paul*, the Americans successfully challenged the dominance of their rivals. But the challenge faded and was not properly renewed until 1952 when the 53,000-ton super-liner, *United States*, came into service and proved a formidable rival to the 'Queens'.

PASSENGERS AND EMIGRANTS: MODES OF TRAVEL

The emigrant trade was highly competitive, which in turn forced the price of tickets down and down. Cunard charged £8.8s in 1860 but this went as low as £3.3s in some ships in the 1880s. Low prices made it imperative to increase the numbers of passengers carried and this gave impetus to the building of larger and larger ships. On average the size of passenger ships during this era increased by 3000 tons every decade, and though some of this space was alloted to luxuries, such as libraries and smoking rooms for those travelling in cabins, most went to increasing the number of steerage passengers.

The increase in carrying capacity made the transport of emigrants travelling steerage a more profitable business than catering for cabin-class passengers; so, as the century progressed, the accommodation for steerage passengers steadily improved. In the 1840s the squalor in which they had been forced to travel had been truly appalling, and death was a not infrequent occurrence. Their only food was a communal potato pot and their sleeping accommodation was wherever they could find a corner for their bedding—which they had to bring themselves. Throughout most of the nineteenth century they were a world apart from the cabin passengers. 'The passengers of the First and Second Class,' read one shipboard notice, 'are requested not to throw money or eatables to the steerage passengers, thereby creating disturbance and annoyance.' By the 1890s some steerage passengers still had to supply their own bedding and eating utensils but at least there were bunks, and most ships provided stewards.

While those in the steerage class fended for themselves as best they could, passengers in the cabin class were pampered and cossetted with every possible delicacy, as a list of food and drink for them on the *Etruria*, during one voyage in 1887, shows:

850 lb of lamb
350 lb of veal
600 fowls
300 chickens
100 ducks
50 geese
80 turkeys
200 brace of grouse
11,500 eggs
220 quarts of ice cream
1100 bottles of champagne

2500 bottles of porter
850 bottles of claret
640 bottles of various spirits
4500 bottles of mineral waters

As competition increased throughout the nineteenth century, passengers began to expect higher and higher standards, so that by the 1870s the cabin-class traveller lived in a style very close to that of a top-class hotel ashore. The Oceanic Steam Navigation Company, known as the White Star Line, was at the forefront in providing this new type of luxury liner. For example, the *Oceanic*, launched in 1870, was the first of a whole string of iron-built, multi-decked passenger ships where, for extra comfort, the saloon was positioned amidships, the cabins were larger, and electric bells could summon a solicitous steward in no time at all. This new type of ship cut the crossing time to under eight days and represented severe competition for other lines, such as Cunard.

To meet this challenge Cunard ordered two new ships, the *Bothnia* (1874) and *Scythia* (1875), both of which were larger than the White Star liners, but were not as fast. These were followed in the early 1880s by the *Servia*—the first steel-hulled liner to serve on the Atlantic route—and the *Aurania*, both of which set new standards of comfort. Then came the *Umbria* and the *Etruria*, the first liners on the North Atlantic run to be fitted with refrigerating machinery. At over 8000 tons gross they werre nearly twice the size of the *Bothnia* and *Scythia*. A booklet which was published to advertise them showed that the new liners catered for the hungry with first-class passengers being offered sustenance throughout the day:

Before breakfast: grapes, melons, etc.
Breakfast: 'Almost anything on earth'
11 am: pint cup of bouillon
Noon: sandwiches carried about the decks
1 pm: lunch
3 pm: trays of ices
4 pm: tea
5 pm: toffee or sweets carried round on trays
7 pm: dinner
9 pm: supper

The same pamphlet also gave judicious advice to lady passengers, which included such tips as sewing coins into hems of skirts so that the sea breezes did not reveal too much,

and that ladies should not sit on deck at night, especially when travelling alone.

A comment from the novelist Mark Twain—that Cunard were so hard-headed and unromantic that they would not have allowed even Noah on board one their ships as First Mate until he had worked his way up to that position—shows that the company's reputation for safety and reliability was now well established. But until the launching of the 12,950-ton *Campania* in 1895 no concerted attempt was made to woo passengers by making luxury a strong selling point. Even as late as 1903 a steerage passenger complained that his accommodation was dirty, smelly and overcrowded, and that the average traveller was made to feel that the company 'was doing him a personal favour in conveying him across the Atlantic.' A reorganization did follow, so that by the time the *Lusitania* and *Mauretania*, were in service in 1907, standards had much improved—so much so indeed that by the outbreak of the First World War Cunard had gained the reputation for luxury for which it is still known today.

STEEL CONSTRUCTION AND SUPER-LINERS

The three decades prior to the outbreak of the First World War saw an era of unique development for liners. During the 1880s iron gave way to steel in the construction of steamships, which reduced their weight without any corresponding loss in strength. By 1890 twin screws were the norm, and quadruple expansion engines further increased both speed and economy; these were followed by the introduction of the steam turbine. As a matter of comparison the Cunard passenger steamer, *Oregon*, held the prized Atlantic Blue Riband in 1884 as did the same company's *Mauretania* in 1914. The 7375-ton *Oregon* had accommodation for 1100 passengers and a single-screw propeller which was driven by three-cylinder compound engines that developed 13,575 hp. Her record crossing took 6 days, 10 hours, 10 minutes; while the 31,938-ton *Mauretania*, which accommodated 2165 passengers, and whose quadruple propellers were driven by steam turbines developing 70,000 total shaft hp, crossed in 4 days, 17 hours, 21 minutes.

The *Mauretania* and her sister ship the *Lusitania* were the first super-liners. They both came into service in 1907 having been built with the help of funds from the British Government which had, reluctantly, come to the aid of Cunard when the Line had been in danger of being absorbed into the vast shipping empire of the American magnate, Junius Morgan. The Government was also anxious to reverse the unpalatable fact that in the matter of passenger liners, at least, Britannia no longer ruled the waves, having been overtaken by the Germans, who were now part of the Morgan shipping combine.

The Government approved a loan and a subsidy and both were given on the understanding that the two ships would be able to maintain 24½ knots in moderate weather, that Cunard would stay British owned, and that the Government would have certain rights over the ships in time of war. The *Lusitania* was torpedoed in 1915, but the *Mauretania* had a long and fruitful life, and was not broken up until 1935. A third liner, the 45,646-ton *Aquitania*, was launched in 1914. These three were by far the biggest, fastest, most luxurious passenger ships ever built up to that time; so large that their passengers hardly realized they were on water at all. 'The main consideration,' said one marine historian, 'is to convey the idea that one is not at sea, but on terra firma.'

Social Manners and Romance

It was aboard these super-liners that the tradition began for first-class passengers to dress for dinner. It was on the first-class decks that the romance of a transatlantic voyage—'the only way to cross'—blossomed and became legend. Advertising by shipping companies often encompassed this romantic dream where all a passenger had to do was buy a ticket and he or she would be wafted aboard a seaborne palace where all their dreams would come true. 'Passengers will remember how romantically the glowing phosphorescent waves curled back in the ship's wake,' wrote a Cunard copywriter, 'falling forever in flakes of diamond and pearl. They will remember how readily the damsel of their choice could be persuaded to a secluded spot in order to observe this poetic phenomenon. They will remember quite a lot of things, we have no doubt.' No doubt they did, and if their memories failed them their imaginations did not.

But though these great liners encouraged an air of both romanticism and detachment from the mundane routine of life ashore, the social manners of the day were still observed. For example, if someone wished to meet a fellow passenger when there was no mutual acquaintance to make the introduction, it was necessary to employ a great deal of tact. One expert in etiquette suggested that if you wanted to introduce yourself to a Mrs Brown, say, not only because you knew her sister but because she was both pretty and travelling alone, you would approach the problem thus. Finding that you were together on the promenade deck you would turn to her and say: 'Mrs Brown, I saw your name in the passenger list and I am going to ask you to let me introduce myself to you on the strength of my long acquaintance with and great affection for your sister, Mrs William Barr, of Cleveland.'

It was always the Captain who was the social arbiter aboard his ship, for it was always he who—with the help of 'Who's Who' and perhaps a note from the Company's head office—picked who should sit at his table during the voyage. It was always his role, according to one Captain:

to adjust disputes, pacify angry women, comfort frightened ones, and judge correctly just when to send one whose conduct is questionable to her room for the rest of the passage. He must know when to forbid the bartender to serve more liquor to a passenger who is drinking too much and just when to post the notice in the smoking room that gamblers are on board.

International Competition

The success of the two Cunard liners spurred the White Star Line—now owned by Morgan, who had also bought up the American Line and several others—into ordering two even larger vessels, the 45,324-ton *Olympic* and her sister ship the *Titanic*.

When she was launched in 1911, the *Olympic* was by far the largest liner in the world, and was the last word in luxury. Her first-class passengers enjoyed all the amenities that Edwardian England could provide, which included a swimming pool, Turkish baths, and a rackets court.

For a short while White Star reigned supreme, but the sinking of the *Titanic* with heavy loss of life after hitting an iceberg in April 1912 led to a slow but steady decline in the fortunes of the line. Eventually, after four years of negotiations, Cunard bought the company in January 1934 and renamed itself Cunard White Star Ltd.

The first years of the century saw an ever-increasing number of immigrants flooding into the New World—1,200,000 entered the United States in 1907 alone—but this flow was curtailed by the US Government after the First World War. To counter this drop in business the phrase 'steerage class' was discarded by shipping lines and accommodation upgraded and renamed 'Tourist Third Cabin', implying respectability, frugality, and privacy. It was spartan, but clean and airy, and was used by the growing number of tourists, most of them American teachers and students, or immigrants whose financial success in their adopted country enabled them to return to Europe to visit friends and relatives.

While Cunard slowly established itself other shipping lines were being founded to trade and carry passengers to every part of the world, and to challenge Cunard's supremacy on the North Atlantic route. Four of the most successful European companies were the Hamburg-Amerika Line and the North German Lloyd Line—which merged to become the HAPAG-Lloyd Line in the early 1930s—the Italia Line and the Compagnie Générale Transatlantique (French Line).

The French Line, based at Le Havre, did not try to compete with the larger trans-atlantic ships, but relied on the individuality of their vessels to attract customers. In 1912 they put into service a new luxury liner, the 24,000-ton *France*, decorated with great

opulence in the style of Louis XIV. She was a great success and in 1921 she was joined by the 34,000-ton *Paris*; but the line only emerged as a serious rival of Cunard and White Star when the *Ile de France* was put into service in 1927.

The Italia Line was an amalgamation of three Italian companies which, during the 1920s, had been in competition with one another for the transatlantic trade from Italy. In 1932 they were combined by the Italian government and the new companies ran two highly successful liners, the 51,075-ton *Rex* and the 48,502-ton *Conte di Savoia*. Both were luxurious, with the *Conte di Savoia* being the first large Atlantic liner to be fitted with a Sperry stabilizer. This limited the roll of the ship to three degrees either side of the vertical which increased the comfort of passengers considerably.

The two German lines rivalled Cunard on the Atlantic run around the turn of the century and then again in the late 1920s. Encouraged by the Kaiser, who was determined that Germany should become a sea power that could rival Great Britain, in 1897 North German Lloyd had launched the largest and fastest ship in the world (at that time): the 14,350-ton *Kaiser Wilhelm der Grosse*. Three years later the Hamburg-Amerika Line introduced the *Deutschland*, which was even faster, and later the *Amerika*, *Imperator*, and *Vaterland*, all larger and faster than their competitors.

The *Amerika* was a milestone along the road of luxury, and became the most fashionable liner on the transatlantic route until the appearance of the *Lusitania* in 1907. She was the first to have her interior created by Charles Mewès who had designed the Ritz hotels in London and Paris. She was also the first liner to be equipped with a lift, and with an à la carte restaurant which was run by the staff of the Ritz-Carlton.

Although the North Atlantic route was the most lucrative, many shipping companies were also founded during the late nineteenth and the early twentieth centuries to trade with other parts of the world. There are too many to mention all of them by name, but South America was served from Britain alone by the Royal Mail Steam Packet Company, the Pacific Steam Navigation Company, the Blue Star Line, the Blue Funnel Line, the Booth Line and the Nelson Line, while the British colonies in South Africa were served by, among others, the Union Line, the Castle Line, and the Diamond Line, the first two merging in 1900 to become the famous Union-Castle Line.

THE 1914–18 WAR AND THE INTER-WAR YEARS

The 1914–18 war was a watershed for many aspects of life, but for those who travelled by sea the pleasures of voyaging to India, Canada, South America, Australia or the

United States, though suspended for more than four years, remained intact to be enjoyed by millions of passengers during the 1920s and 1930s. New technology allowed liners to become faster, quieter, and even more luxurious than pre-war liners. And though no new large liner came into service until the *Ile de France* in 1927, the pre-war ones that had survived the conflict were refurbished and mostly converted to oil burning, which brought in a cleaner and quieter era of travel. The larger German ones were taken from their owners under the terms of the armistice: the 51,969-ton *Imperator* became Cunard's *Berengaria*; the 54,282-ton *Vaterland* was alloted to the United States Lines and became the *Leviathan*; and the 56,551-ton *Bismarck*, which had been launched in June 1914 but not completed until 1922, became the White Star's *Majestic*, and remained the largest liner afloat until the *Normandie* was launched in 1933. Instead, the Hamburg-Amerika Line introduced the much smaller *Albert Ballin* class, and it was not until 1929 that the Germans began to compete against the North Atlantic giants with the launch of North German Lloyd's *Bremen*.

Another line to suffer heavily from the 1914–18 war was P&O. In 1914 it had managed to consolidate its position by merging with British India, the largest shipping line east of Suez, but many of its ships were sunk and it took time to replace them. Nevertheless, during the 1920s it did expand and became a worldwide organization, running 500 ships. It bought several shipping lines and a controlling interest in the Orient Line and then launched into a building programme which, besides producing the first ships to exceed 20,000 tons, introduced the highly successful C and R-class liners. Then in 1929 a superb new creation, the *Viceroy of India*, was put into service. Powered by turbo-electric drive, she was the last word in luxury. The first-class smoking room simulated the great hall of a castle, complete with hammerbeams, crossed swords on the walls, and a huge fireplace with baronial arms above it, while the swimming pool—P&O's first—was decorated with copies of Pompeiian reliefs. Yet even this luxury was soon eclipsed when, between 1931 and 1938, the company put into service the five liners whose names all started with *Strath*. Every first-class cabin had hot and cold running water, there was rudimentary air conditioning, and their speed brought the journey to Bombay down to 15 days.

By the 1920s the craze for listening to gramophone records and dancing to bands had begun to replace the impromptu sing-song or amateur concert, and for the first time since 1881 no music room was provided in a P&O ship. Instead, there was a reading and writing room, and a verandah cafe. Throughout the inter-war period, in fact, on-board entertainment slowly changed from being arranged by the passengers themselves to being on a more organized basis. Silly games were relegated to the children's parties and

were replaced by more adult pastimes like deck tennis, swimming, sunbathing, dancing, and playing what we now know as bingo.

The *Ile de France*
The first large transatlantic liner to be built after the First World War was the 43,500-ton *Ile de France*, launched for the French Line in March 1926. With her modern decor and exquisite cuisine, she became an immediate success, and, indeed, a legend. She was built for elegance and good living, not for speed, and that was how her passengers liked it. During one crossing the *Mauretania* raced past her just as her passengers were sitting down to dinner. Some left their tables to watch the great liner going by but one old gentlemen continued to eat with great relish. Minutes later he was brought a radio telegram from a friend aboard the Cunarder. 'Do you want a tow?' it read. The old gourmet laid down his knife and fork and scribbled the following reply: 'No thank you stop what's your hurry? stop Are you starving?' The *Ile* crossed the Atlantic 347 times before the 1939–45 war intervened, and her distinguished list of passengers included such names as Arturo Toscanini, Maurice Chevalier, Tallulah Bankhead, Gloria Swanson and Barbara Hutton. Anyone who was anyone travelled on the *Ile* and made sure that everyone else knew about it.

Although the atmosphere on the *Ile de France* was something new to be savoured, the first real advance in design came with the 51,656-ton *Bremen*. Her lines included new features like the bulbous bow beneath the waterline, which increased speed (because it cut down on water resistance to the hull) and a streamlined superstructure and funnels. Her 732 first-class passengers travelled in the greatest luxury. Not only did their cabins have hot and cold running water, but the swimming pool was heated too, and other luxurious appointments included a special dining room known as the 'Hunt Room' which was decorated with tapestries. For several years the *Bremen* and her sister ship the *Europa*—which after the 1939–45 war became the French-run *Liberté*—held the Blue Riband and attracted a sizeable percentage of the North Atlantic passenger trade, and their dominance was only broken by a new breed of thousand-foot super-liners that were constructed in the 1930s.

A New Breed of Liner
The first of this new breed to enter service was the 80,000-ton *Normandie* built for the French Line. She made her maiden voyage to New York in May 1935, and, having exceeded 32 knots during her trials, easily broke the record and gained the Blue Riband. She carried only 1972 passengers in a variety of classes, which included 28 *de grand luxe*

suites each consisting of five or six rooms and 30 de luxe suites which had two rooms each. The first-class accommodation was hardly less luxurious, there being 24 veranda suites, each for two or three people, as well as ordinary staterooms. All had private baths and telephones. The public rooms included an air-conditioned dining saloon capable of taking 700 people at one sitting, a chapel, a hospital, shops, swimming pools, a cinema/theatre, and a winter garden with fountains, aquaria, and large cages full of singing birds. She was, according to one historian of passenger liners, probably the greatest ship ever built anywhere.

Hard on the heels of the *Normandie* came Cunard's latest creation, the 81,235-ton *Queen Mary*, and these two floating luxury hotels shared the Blue Riband between them until the outbreak of war. 'The French built a beautiful hotel and put a ship around it', one observer remarked; 'the British built a beautiful ship and put a hotel inside it.'

Ever since the late 1920s Cunard had been planning an 80,000-ton super-liner, but the Great Depression had delayed her construction and the *Queen Mary* did not leave Southampton on her maiden voyage until March 1936. At 1019 feet overall, she was ten feet shorter than the *Normandie* but was just as lavishly furnished throughout her 12 decks; and her 2139 passengers travelled as if they were accommodated at the Ritz. The amount of food and drink she carried for just one voyage was staggering, and included 106 tons of beef, 25 tons of potatoes, 18 tons of vegetables, a ton of sausages, half a ton of tea, 70,000 eggs, 1000 jars of jam, 2½ tons of bacon, 160 gallons of salad oil, 2000 gallons of ice cream, nine tons of fish, half a ton of bananas, 500 lb of smoked salmon, and 4½ tons of lamb. The amount of drink was equally lavish, with 2500 bottles of whisky, 6000 bottles of beer and 3000 bottles of wine being consumed, with a million and a half cigarettes and 15,000 cigars smoked. Another interesting statistic was the fact that out of 1101 officers and men aboard the *Queen Mary*, only 351 were employed in actually running the ship, the rest being there solely to cater to the passengers' every whim.

The inter-war period marked the apogee of the era of liner travel. The rich and the famous all travelled on the great ocean greyhounds and were seen from the publicity photographs to be doing so. Royalty, politicians, film stars, sports personalities, and millionaire businessmen all added their individual glamour to the aura that surrounded these great floating luxury hotels. When the Prince of Wales boarded the *Ile de France* he brought with him 135 pieces of luggage; and one renowned American woman crossed frequently with ten maids and four cars. The baron of beef in the first-class dining room of the *Majestic* on Christmas day weighed 334 lb. Everything, in fact, was all a little larger than life, and that was just how everyone wanted it to be.

THE POST-WAR ERA

The 1939–45 war put a stop to all the fun, of course, and when the companies tried to revive the frivolousness and luxury afterwards it was not quite the same. The war hit P&O even harder than the first conflict. It again suffered severe losses to its fleet, and recovery after the war was slow; changed circumstances meant more emphasis on cargo carrying and less on passengers. Its first postwar liner was the 27,955-ton *Himalaya*, launched in 1949 for the Australian run, which became increasingly important once India became independent. She was followed by the *Oriana* and then by the 45,500-ton *Canberra*, one of the few unconventional liners the P&O has ever built. Launched in 1960, the *Canberra* could carry 2250 passengers in style, and is still doing so, but after the Suez Canal was closed by war in 1967 the Line ceased to run a scheduled service to the Far East and Australia.

On that most glamorous of routes, the North Atlantic run, efforts were made, despite the shortages, to return the liners to their former glory. For a while it worked. The 83,673-ton *Queen Elizabeth*, a troopship throughout the war after being launched in 1940, certainly brought, with the *Queen Mary*, a brief sparkle to a dull, post-war world, a temporary haven from the drabness of Socialism and rationing, and later a leisurely alternative to the increasingly frenetic world of commercial flying. But by the 1960s the ships had become dingy, reminding one writer of the increasingly deserted British seaside resorts of the time, with the service becoming less than immaculate. The *Queen Mary* was sold first, in 1967, to become a tourist attraction at Long Beach, California, and was followed by the *Queen Elizabeth* in 1968. She was destined to become a convention centre but her new owners went broke. She was bought by a Hong Kong shipping magnate who planned to turn her into a floating university, but she caught fire and sank in Hong Kong harbour: a sad end to two fine ships.

During this postwar period the French produced another superb liner, the *France*, the British had the two Queens, the Americans the *United States*, but the age of the jet finished them all. Even the appearance of the *QEII* in 1969 could not turn the tide, and if you want to be on a scheduled crossing of the Atlantic now you have to be on one 35,000 feet above the ocean.

But the liner is not finished, not by any means, for while the scheduled passenger ship is a thing of the past, the cruise liner has taken its place. A lot of the glamour has gone, and all the exclusivity, but the sea still attracts many thousands of passengers every year. For some it is still the only way to travel.

A HISTORY
IN PHOTOGRAPHS

3 *(left) The first transatlantic Cunarder, the 1135-ton wooden paddle steamer, Britannia, which was launched in 1840 and inaugurated the first regular Atlantic mail service by steamer. Vessels carrying the Royal Mail were obliged to carry at least one cat as rats tended to nibble the mail bags. Britannia carried three and also had a cow aboard to give passengers fresh milk during the 14-day voyage. For those who enjoyed a stronger tipple, the wine and spirits bar was open between 6 am and 11 pm, and passengers frequently breakfasted on steak and a bottle of hock.*

4 *(above) Accommodation aboard Britannia was spartan. This is the cabin used by Charles Dickens and his wife when they travelled aboard her to America in 1842. The Atlantic voyage was usually rough, as one passenger graphically described: 'At meal times the tables are covered with an oil cloth. This I found to be slippery and in practice full plates tended to slip off into one's lap whenever Britannia rolled—which she did incessantly. The amount of crockery smashed must be of alarm to the owners. I lost count of the number of times that a sharp roll caused the sound of a cascading clatter of breaking china from the pantry next door . . . since the food is carried over open decks it is sometimes cold despite the silver covers. As usual we have fresh food for the first three days and thereafter the fish and meat is salted. Britannia has two ice rooms and the fruit is stored there. At least we are sure of avoiding scurvy!'*

5 *The 2936-ton* Great Britain *designed by Isambard Kingdom Brunel was the first ocean-going passenger ship to be made of iron and to be driven by a propeller, and, like Brunel's earlier* Great Western, *she followed the trend towards luxury which was eventually to become the hallmark of transatlantic travel. 'The walls of the after or principal promenade saloon are painted in delicate tints,' one newspaper wrote of her, 'and along the sides are several fixed chairs of oak. A row of well-proportioned pillars, which range down the centre of the promenade, served the double purpose of ornament to the room and support to the decks. In this saloon, on either side, is a range of exceedingly comfortable state rooms and sleeping berths. About twelve of these on each side of the deck will be reserved for ladies, as they are made to communicate with two commodious ladies' boudoirs, or private sitting rooms, measuring 17 feet by 14 feet.'*

Great Britain *started her maiden voyage across the Atlantic on 26 July 1845 and covered the 3300 miles from Liverpool to New York in just under 15 days. Though she had a capacity for 360 passengers she carried only 50, as people were still a little afraid of her size.*

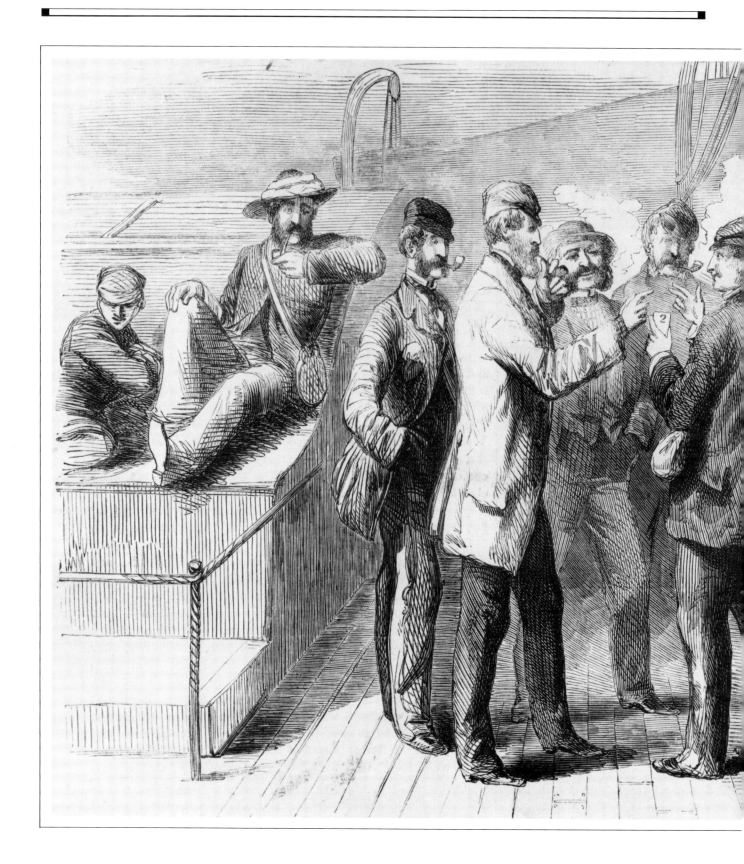

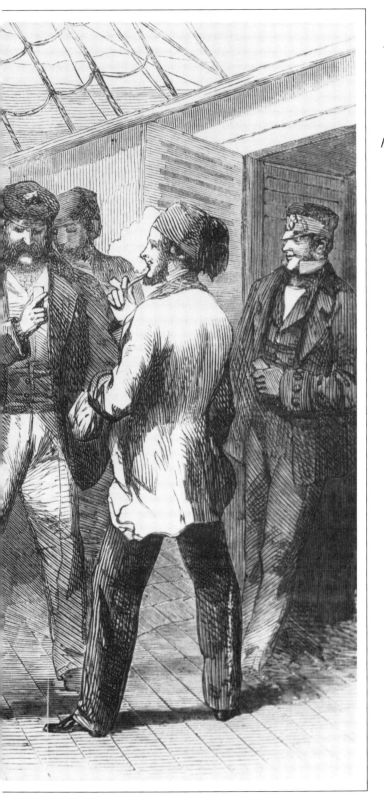

6 *Early P&O passengers had to be transported from Alexandria to Suez by river-steamer to Cairo and then to Suez to meet their P&O ship which would transport them to their final destinations. Their luggage was taken by camel from Alexandria to Suez and often arrived badly knocked about. Passengers travelled to Cairo by river-steamer and then to Suez in crude horse-drawn carriages known as 'vans'. This illustration, drawn about 1855, shows passengers aboard a P&O steamer, Valetta, drawing lots for which 'vans' were to leave Cairo first.*

7 *The 2021-ton P&O steamer Ceylon of 1858. These scenes drawn for the Graphic magazine show the dining saloon, the ladies' boudoir, and the deck looking forward.*

8 *On the poop of a P&O steamer in the Red Sea during the 1860s. The awning which can be seen in this illustration would have protected the passengers from the worst of the searing heat, but it was never a pleasant experience. 'Your eyes were dry and sore and your lips cracked like withered leaves,' one passenger recorded of an early voyage. 'Standing was worse than sitting, and lying down was worse than either. Talking withered your throat; and keeping silence wearied your soul. Sleep was but a restless struggle with a red-hot nightmare, and walking but a fevered sleep.'*

9 *This illustration from the* Graphic, *dated 10 April 1875, shows visitors leaving the 2202-ton P&O steamer* Sumatra *just before its departure from Southampton for India. P&O did not carry emigrants and in those days its passengers were normally civil servants, businessmen, and army officers, who travelled first class, and their servants who travelled second class. Clergymen and missionaries, who were invariably impecunious, also travelled second class.*

10 *The Sunday service has always been part of shipboard life and was attended by all on board. Normally it was conducted by the ship's captain. This illustration from the Graphic of 10 April 1875 shows the captain of the Sumatra taking the service under the shade of the ship's awning.*

▐▐ *Bad weather was a real hazard for early passenger liners and shipwrecks caused by navigational error or storms were not infrequent. As can be seen in this illustration from the* Graphic *of 10 April 1875, titled 'A Glimpse of the Sun', the ship's officers of the 2431-ton P&O liner,* Zambesi, *are trying to take a sun sight with their sextants while watching passengers hang on as best they can—or slip.*

12 *The P&O liner,* Rome, *launched in 1881. Along with her sister ship,* Carthage, *she was the first P&O ship to exceed 5000 tons. These were also the first to have the second-class accommodation aft, over the propeller; and to have the first-class accommodation in the middle, where there was less movement and noise. They were both designed for the Australian service.*

13 *Passengers relaxing aboard the* Rome, *while ever-helpful stewards hover near them. It was not always so tranquil, as the decks were often used for games or other forms of entertainment. 'On Thursday and Friday afternoons', wrote one passenger, 'the various committees appointed were busily engaged in carrying out the sports arranged. Quoits, bull, potato race, egg-and-spoon race, tugs-of-war, skipping contests, thread-needle races, etc., in addition to chess, whist, euchre, cribbage tournaments provided an abundance of amusements.'*

14 *(left) Passengers sheltering from the breeze aboard the 7269-ton Cunard liner, Aurania. This was probably taken on her maiden voyage from Liverpool to New York in June 1883, as her engines failed in mid-Atlantic and she had to make the rest of the voyage under sail. She had accommodation for 480 first-class and 700 third-class passengers.*

15 *(above) When the 8120-ton Cunard liner, Umbria, seen here, and her sister ship, Etruria, were launched in 1884, they outclassed all their transatlantic rivals in size and capacity. They were also the first Cunarders to have refrigeration machinery.*

16 *A first class stateroom aboard* Umbria *which approached the luxury of a first-class hotel ashore. She initially carried 550 first-class and 800 third-class passengers, but berths for 160 intermediate passengers were added later. Her route was Liverpool–Queenstown–New York.*

17 *The 7558-ton* Caledonia. *At the time she was constructed, 1894, she was the largest ship in the P&O fleet. In the following year she broke the outward record to Bombay and on her voyage home easily best the Messageries Maritimes steamer* Ernest Simon, *which had been specially designed to outrun P&O ships.*

18 *The promenade deck of the Caledonia. Although a lot more comfortable than earlier P&O steamers, travelling in the* Caledonia *was hardly luxurious, as an account by one of its assistant pursers reveals: 'There were very few single-berth cabins, and those were on the top deck, the remainder contained two or three berths, and in the Second Saloon even four berths. It was always a puzzle to me how all the passengers settled in amicably, as there was very little room for furniture which was only sparsely provided. The main item was a weird arrangement like a coffin standing on end; on the top it had a bracket to hold a glass for drinking water and two tumblers, a hole to pour water into a tank which was faced by a looking glass, and underneath this a basin could be let down, exposing a tap. There was no other furniture except a camp stool. Passengers kept whatever they wanted to use during their voyage in their cabin trunks stowed under the bunks. . . . There was no provision for ventilation in the cabins, or any means of heating.'*

19 *The 7661-ton* Auguste Victoria *passing the Statue of Liberty. Launched in 1889 she was a typical Hamburg-Amerika liner of her period, carrying 400 first-class, 120 second-class, and 580 third-class passengers in ornate luxury between Hamburg, Southampton and New York.*

20 *The music room aboard the* Auguste Victoria.

21 *(above) The ladies' saloon aboard the* Auguste Victoria.

22 *(right) By the end of the nineteenth century carrying emigrants to the United States had become big business. Here emigrants are being picked up from their lodgings in Liverpool before boarding the Cunard liner* Lucania. *The date is 1895.*

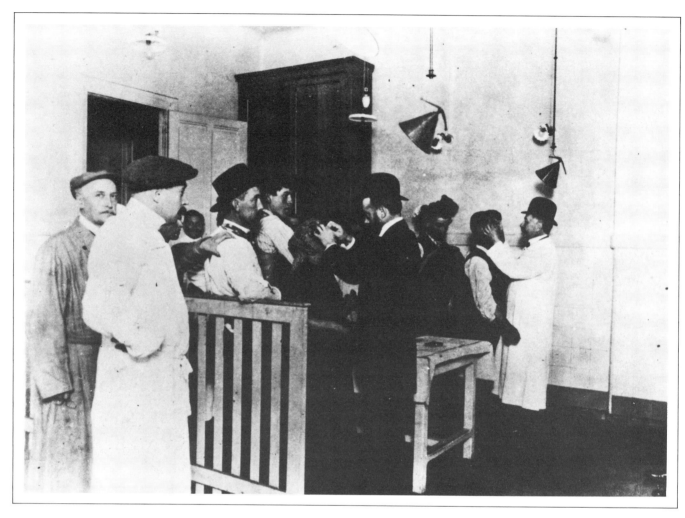

23 *Doctors inspecting emigrants at Le Havre for trachoma
before they board their ship for the New World.*

24 *Emigrants queueing up for a meal aboard the 12,830-
ton transatlantic liner* Graf Waldersee. *Until quite late on
they had to provide their own utensils. The* Graf Waldersee,
*launched in 1899, was owned by the Hamburg-Amerika
Line and could carry 2200 emigrants as well as 162 first-
class and 184 second-class passengers, between Hamburg
and New York via Boulogne. She was one of many liners
which carried emigrants around the turn of the century.*

25 *While emigrants were crammed aboard transatlantic liners, first-class passengers enjoyed every luxury. Here are a group aboard the* Graf Waldersee *playing deck quoits, always a popular game aboard ship. Note the steward in attendance carrying spare quoits.*

26 *Mothers hoping their daughters might make a good catch during the long voyage to India would often send them P&O to relatives in India. They were commonly known as the 'fishing fleet'.*

Seen here are two lady passengers with Captain Loggin, the Commander of the 6500-ton P&O steamer Arcadia. The photograph was taken in 1894, some 22 years after the Company issued a circular to officers instructing them not to be overfamiliar with passengers. Obviously Captain Loggin not only thought himself exempt from this instruction but also that he deserved to get his feet up occasionally.
The Arcadia marked a significant advance in size, comfort and elegance, compared with the rest of the P&O fleet, when she was built in 1887. Her bathrooms were particularly luxurious, for the baths were of solid marble and had hot and cold salt water, spray and showers, while the bunks were all fitted with patent spring mattresses.

27 *By the early 1900s the two German lines of Hamburg-Amerika and North German Lloyd dominated the Atlantic run. The Hamburg-Amerika 16,502-ton liner* Deutschland, *launched in 1900, was especially popular. She was the Line's only record breaker, crossing the Atlantic at an average speed of 22.42 knots. She carried 450 first-class, 300 second-class, and 350 third-class passengers.*

28 *A cross section of the* Deutschland.

30 *(right)* An austere third-class cabin on the Cunard liner Carmania, *which was launched in 1905. Although only 19,524 tons she could carry 2000 third-class passengers in cabins like this one.*

29 *(above)* The interior of the Deutschland *was designed by the creator of the Ritz hotels in London and Paris, Charles Mewès. This is the dining saloon, a typical example of the ostentatiousness which all Hamburg-Amerika liners of the period showed.*

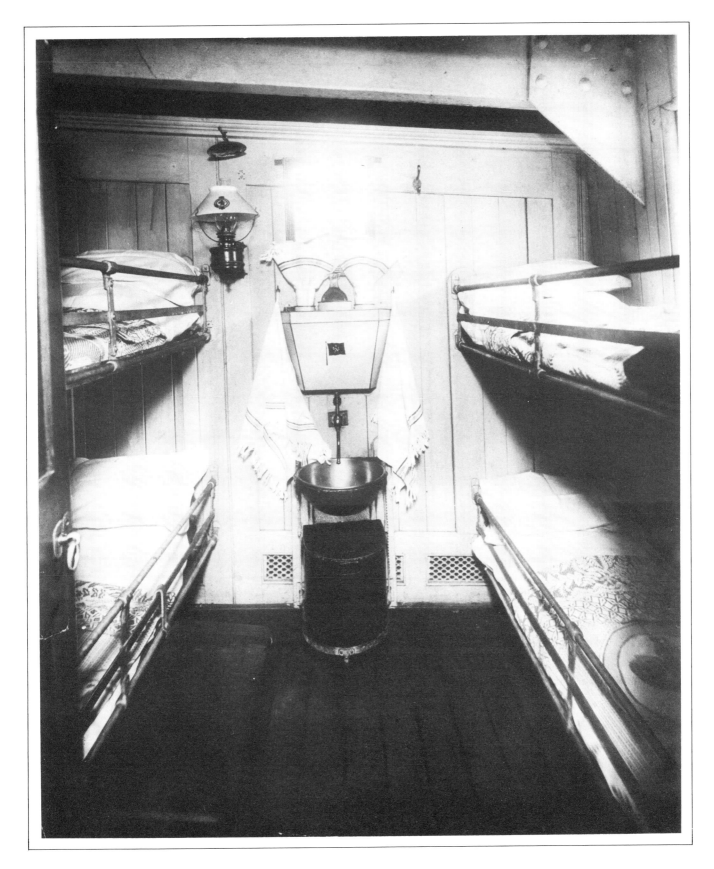

31 *By 1907 the Cunard Line had recaptured domination of the North Atlantic run from the Germans with the launching of two new quadruple-screw super-liners:* Lusitania *(31,550 tons), seen here docked at Liverpool, and* Mauretania *(31,938 tons). The latter was not scrapped until 1935, but the* Lusitania *was sunk by a German U-boat in 1915 with heavy loss of life.*

32 *The 51,969-ton* Imperator, *owned by Hamburg-Amerika, was the Germans' reply to the White Star's* Olympic. *She was launched in 1912 and carried 4234 passengers in four classes. Those in first class travelled in previously unknown luxury, many of them in luxury suites with private sitting room and bathroom. After the 1914–18 war she became Cunard's* Berengaria.

33 *(left) Advertisement for* Imperator.

34 *(above) The swimming pool of* Imperator *designed by Charles Mewès was a copy of the one he designed for the Royal Automobile Club in London. It had marble columns and reached through two decks.*

35 *The winter garden aboard the* Imperator, *positioned at one end of the Ritz-Carlton grill.*

36 *At the beginning of the century smokers—and they were only men—were made to indulge their habit in smoking rooms. Here some Germanic-looking gentlemen enjoy a cigar and a glass of beer in the smoking room of the* Imperator. *Note the heavy wooden panelling.*

37 *The* Festhalle *of the* Imperator *where every first-class passenger gathered to have tea and gossip about the other passengers.*

38 *(left) The Hamburg-Amerika* Vaterland, *launched months before the outbreak of the 1914–18 war, was an improved* Imperator *and, at 54,282 tons, slightly larger. She is seen here in the docks at Cuxhaven. She was seized by the Americans in 1917, renamed the* Leviathan, *and was used on the Atlantic run between the wars until she was scrapped in 1938.*

39 *(above) Dancing in the* Festhalle *of the* Vaterland.

40 *The ladies, modestly attired, enjoying a dip in the
swimming pool of the* Vaterland.

41 *While the ladies played in the swimming pool the gentleman guests aboard* Vaterland *enjoyed the ease of the sauna.*

42 *The famous 45,647-ton Cunarder* Aquitania, *launched in 1914 and seen here in Sydney harbour during the 1939–45 war, was used in both world wars to transport troops and as a hospital ship.*

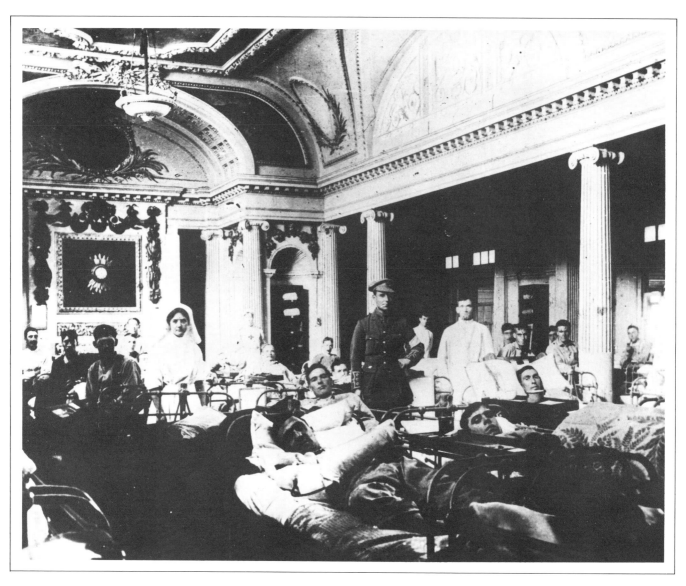

43 *Survivors from the Dardenelles landings, 1915, aboard the* Aquitania.

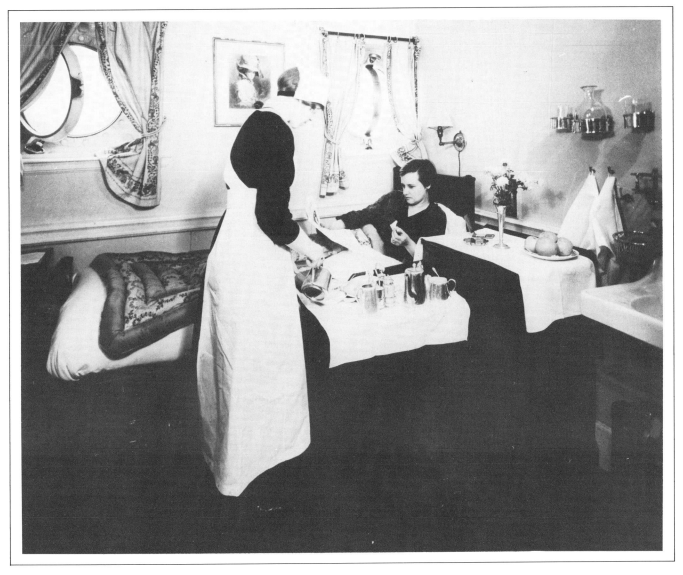

44 *After the 1914–18 war* Aquitania *was converted to oil burning and became, during the 1920s, one of the most popular transatlantic liners. Here a passenger in a second-class stateroom enjoys breakfast in bed.*

45 *The young flappers of the 1920s and their partners at an afternoon tea dance aboard Aquitania. The date of this photograph is 27 May 1927.*

46 *Second-class passengers aboard* Aquitania *having afternoon tea in the winter sunshine. This photograph was taken in February 1928.*

47 *A pet show aboard the Aquitania in 1932.*

48 *Passengers boarding the 16,000-ton P&O liner* Naldera *at Tilbury just after the 1914–18 war. She was one of the first ships the Company acquired after the First World War.*

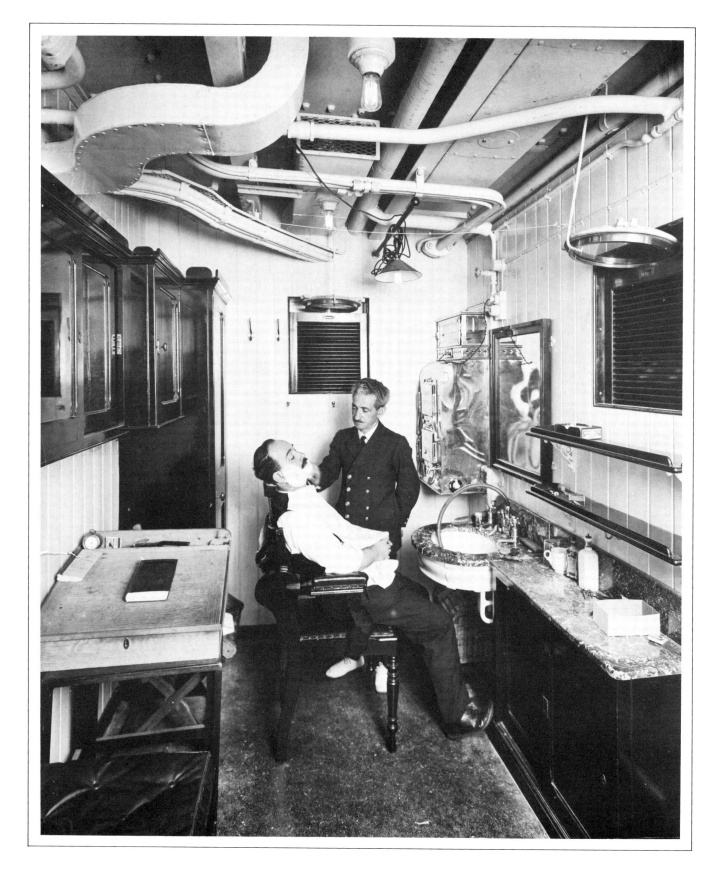

49 *(left) A morning shave for a passenger in the barber's shop aboard the Royal Mail Line's 22,181-ton* Alcantara II, *launched in 1927 for the Southampton–Buenos Aires route.*

50 *(above) After the 1914–18 war the Hamburg-Amerika Line replaced the liners they had lost with smaller ships, including those of the 'Albert Ballin' class. This is the first of them, the 20,815-ton* Albert Ballin, *named after the famous director of the Line. She is seen here leaving Cuxhaven soon after her launch in 1923.*

51 *A first-class suite in the* Albert Ballin.

52 *The first-class writing room in the* Albert Ballin.

53 *(left)* *The shop aboard the* Albert Ballin. **54** *(above)* *The tourist-class dining room aboard the* Albert Ballin.

55 *Another of the 'Albert Ballin' class was the 21,455-ton*
New York, *seen here leaving Cuxhaven. She was launched in*
1926.

56 *A first-class cabin aboard* New York.

57 *The cinema was an entirely new entertainment for the passengers of transatlantic liners during the 1920s. Here, first-class passengers aboard* New York *watch a film of the liner being docked. The screen has been set up in the ship's* Festhalle.

58 *A Hamburg-Amerika illustration of what was needed aboard a liner of the 'Albert Ballin' class to wine and dine the 1700 passengers and crew.*

59 *The first large transatlantic liner to be built after the 1914–18 war was the French Line's 45,000-ton* Ile de France, *launched in 1926. Seen here punching her way through an Atlantic gale, the* Ile *became a popular ship with the young set. Anyone who was anyone travelled on her.*

60 *All the elegance of the Ile de France can be seen in this photograph of exquisite couples enjoying themselves on the dance floor.*

61 *(above) What was appealing about the* Ile de France *was not just her elegance but the fact that she was bang up to date. She was one of the few transatlantic liners to have her own mail plane, seen here about to be launched; and she was the first, in 1928, to inaugurate a regular air mail service with a plane which could carry six passengers. (The first mail plane ever launched from a liner flew from the* Leviathan *in August 1927.)*

62 *(right) Shuffleboard being playing aboard a Cunard liner during the 1920s. It has always been a favourite deck game for passengers.*

63 *Another favourite pastime for passengers has always been deck quoits. Here a small group play, rather inaccurately, on the deck of the 20,158-ton Cunard liner Franconia, which was launched in 1923. She carried 330 first-class, 420 second-class, and 950 third-class passengers between Liverpool (or Southampton) and New York. She survived the 1939–45 war as a troopship and was eventually scrapped in 1956.*

64 *Another perennial favourite pastime on ocean liners has always been the tug-of-war. Here, passengers aboard the 18,724-ton* Laurentic *have been divided up into the Widowers vs the Merry Widows, which no doubt later stimulated some shipboard romances—perhaps the most popular pastime of all aboard passenger ships. The* Laurentic *was launched in 1927 for the White Star Line but became part of the Cunard fleet when the two lines were amalgamated in 1934.*

65 *P&O had always relied on comfort and reliability more than sheer luxury to attract customers. But with the 19,648-ton* Viceroy of India, *launched in 1929, the company 'went overboard', and she was lavishly fitted out. Powered by turbo-electric drive, she was not only fast but extremely quiet. A unique feature of her accommodation was that all first-class passengers had single-berth cabins, most of which could be turned into suites by opening a communicating door.*

66 *(above) Before the* Viceroy of India, *passengers aboard P&O liners had always had to make do with a canvas swimming pool rigged on deck. But the company's glamour ship had a luxury pool called the 'Pompeiian Bath'.*

67 *(right) The first-class smoking room in the* Viceroy of India *was typical of the luxury surrounding her passengers. Designed by Elsie Mackay, a daughter of P&O's chairman, Lord Inchcape, it was in the style of the great hall of a castle, crossed swords and all.*

68 *The 16,385-ton liner* Mongolia, *launched in 1923, was more typical than the* Viceroy of India *of the kind of ship P&O employed between the wars: comfortable but unostentatious.*

69 *The Mongolia's boats packed with passengers looking forward to a few hours ashore at Ceuta.*

70 *Passengers from* Mongolia *thronging the quayside at Ceuta.*

71 *A diving competition in the wood and canvas swimming pool rigged-up aboard* Mongolia *during her voyage to the Far East in 1933.*

72 *Neptune awaiting his victims as* Mongolia *crossed the equator during the 1933 voyage.*

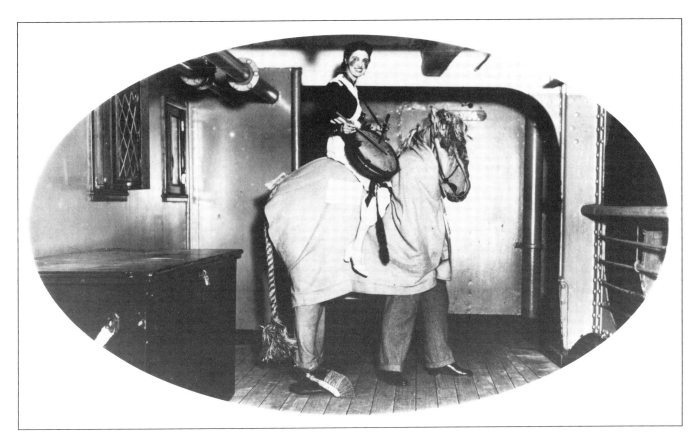

73 *Fancy dress parties and dances were always very much part of the scene on board any liner. Here, Mrs Perrottet is dressed up as the Drummer during a fancy dress dance aboard the* Mongolia, *1933.*

74 *The children's Christmas fancy dress party aboard the*
Mongolia, *1933.*

Purser Roger Raulin

S. A. M. Ile de France

Buster Keaton /
Maurice Chevalier H.3455

75 *The rich and the famous travelled world-wide by sea during the 1920s and 1930s. Here Buster Keaton and Maurice Chevalier sit next to one another at the Purser's table on the* Ile de France.

76 *A publicity photo of the actress Cecile Sorel aboard the Ile de France.*

77 *(above) Ex-Prime Minister David Lloyd George playing quoits aboard a P&O liner during a convalescent trip to Ceylon at the end of 1931.*

78 *(right) The Indian leader, Mahatma Gandhi, posing with the captain of the P&O liner* Rajputana, *in which he travelled to Europe in 1931.*

79 *The actress Phyllis Calvert, with her family, is greeted by photographers when she arrives at Southampton in the Cunard liner* Queen Mary.

80 *Liners were suitably romantic and dramatic locations for making films. Here, Anna Q. Nilsson and Robert Cain are shooting a scene for the film* Too Much Money *aboard the Cunard liner,* Franconia. *Note the cameras above them.*

81 *The first of the thousand-foot liners, the 79,300-ton*
Normandie, *seen here entering New York harbour after her
maiden voyage from Le Havre to New York in May 1935.
She had accommodation for 1972 passengers, which
included 28 de grand luxe suites, some of which contained as
many as six rooms.*

82 *The general theme of the decor aboard the Normandie was the history of Normandy since the eleventh century, which perhaps accounts for the ornate decorations in the first-class chapel.*

83 *The sheer elegance and luxury enjoyed by passengers aboard the* Normandie *is well captured here in this photograph of dinner in the first-class dining room.*

84 *By contrast, the crew of the Normandie ate in the sparsest surroundings, but the food was probably still excellent.*

85 *The vast sun deck of the* Normandie *gave passengers enough room to play any kind of sport they wanted.*

86 *Entertainment for the passengers was laid on day and night aboard the* Normandie. *Here the passengers are entertained by a trapeze artist halfway up the liner's mast.*

87 *Doing the splits in front of first-class passengers during an after-dinner entertainment aboard the* Normandie.

88 *The two Cunard 'Queens'*—Queen Mary *in the foreground—personified the kind of excellence and luxury which transatlantic travel was able to offer passengers just before, and for a few years after, the 1939–45 war.*

89 *(left)* *A Cunard poster showing sailing times for their liners during the last half of the 1930s.*

90 *(above)* *A pre-war photograph of stewardesses on* Queen Mary *lining up for lifeboat drill just before sailing. They are in the shopping centre for first-class passengers, situated on the promenade deck.*

91 *Passengers, too, had to muster for lifeboat drill before
the start of a voyage. This photograph was also taken
aboard the* Queen Mary.

92 *By the 1930s, sunbathing had become perhaps the most popular way of idling through the long days of an ocean voyage. These passengers are on the promenade deck of the HAPAG-Lloyd liner, Milwaukee, in 1936.*

93 Queen Mary *(middle) docked in New York. On her left is* Britannic *and on her right, the second* Mauretania.

94 *Boxing tournaments between crew members were often arranged for passengers. This is one aboard the* Queen Mary.

95 *Between 1931 and 1938 P&O acquired five new liners, all of which achieved a new height in elegance and comfort, and on which second-class passengers became tourist class—which meant in those days that they had the money to tour. All cabins had running water—though only first-class cabins had hot water—and there was rudimentary air conditioning. This is perhaps the most famous of them,* the Stratheden.

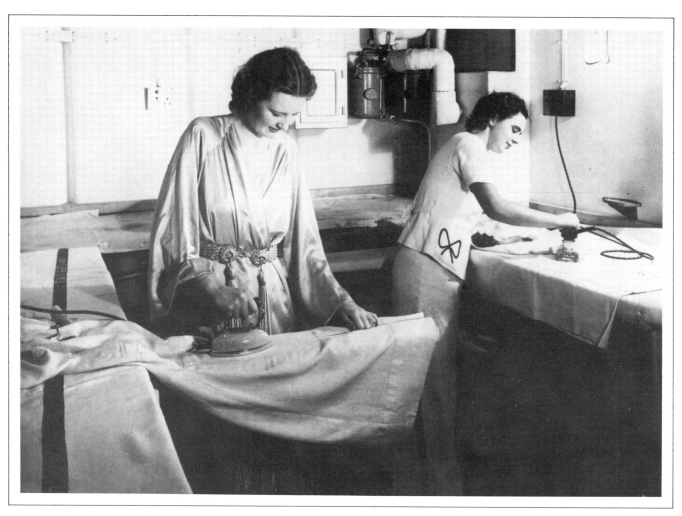

96 *(above) Tourist-class lady passengers doing their
ironing aboard the Stratheden.*

97 *(right) The largest Cunard liner of them all, the
83,673-ton Queen Elizabeth, carried troops before she ever
carried any civilian passengers, as she was not launched
until 1940.*

98 *Bell boys being inspected aboard the* Queen Mary.

99 *After the Second World War the boat trains still ran and the great liners still sailed to ports all over the world. But somehow the glamour had faded, as the rather grim expressions on the faces of these passengers perhaps reflect.*

100 *This cheerless photograph, taken in January 1951, is of the first-class Customs and Baggage Hall at the new ocean passenger terminal at Southampton. Efficient, no doubt, but rather drab. A lot of the excitement had by then gone from travelling by sea.*

101 *Ocean liners have always carried all sort of curious cargoes. Here the 100,000th Ford car to be sold to the United States is loaded aboard the* Queen Mary. *The date is November 1958.*

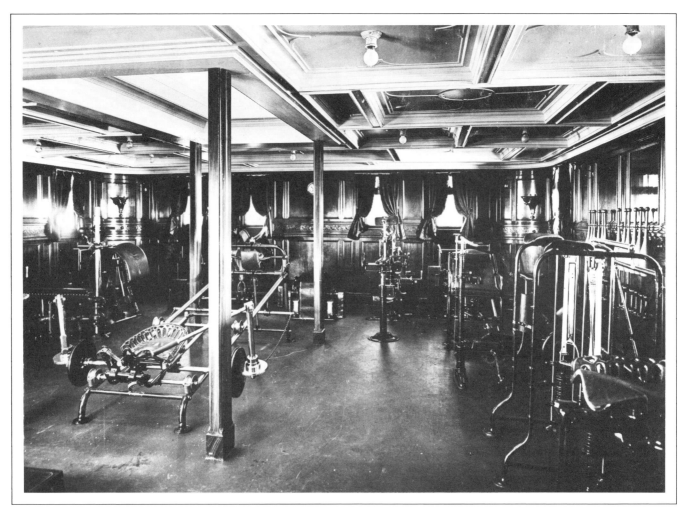

102 *Not a torture chamber, but a gymnasium aboard an early Hamburg-Amerika liner. Compare it with the . . .*

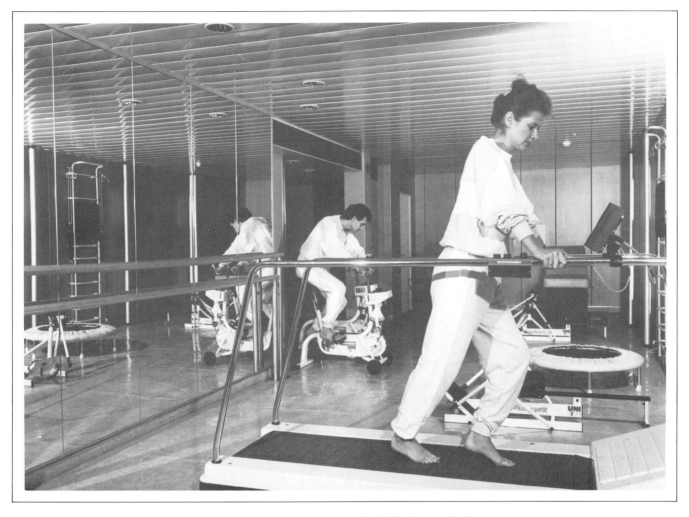

103 . . . *modern fitness centre in HAPAG-Lloyd's latest*
Europa.

104 *Post-war publicity photographs tried to conjure up a glamour which by the late 1950s had, in reality, gone even from the 'Queens'. Here the young Roger Moore, in his days as a male model, poses in a not altogether unsuccessful effort to create an atmosphere of exclusivity and luxury aboard one of the great Cunard liners.*

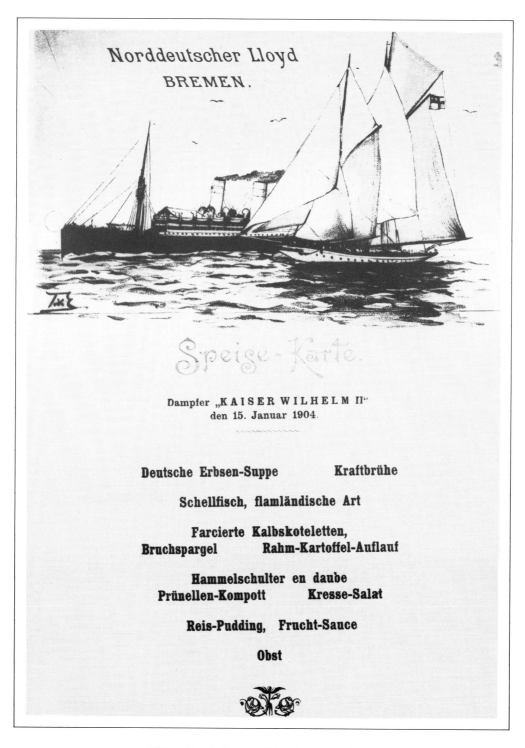

Norddeutscher Lloyd
BREMEN.

Speise-Karte

Dampfer „KAISER WILHELM II"
den 15. Januar 1904.

Deutsche Erbsen-Suppe   Kraftbrühe

Schellfisch, flamländische Art

Farcierte Kalbskoteletten,
Bruchspargel   Rahm-Kartoffel-Auflauf

Hammelschulter en daube
Prünellen-Kompott   Kresse-Salat

Reis-Pudding, Frucht-Sauce

Obst

105 *A North German Lloyd menu c. 1904.*

106 *Hamburg-Amerika Line advertisement.*

The Kids' Tea

A Storm at sea

Professional advice.

Tied in with Tape :
a sketch in the saloon

107 *(left) Wine list, Hamburg-Amerika Line.*

108 *(above) P&O pencillings.*

109 *Royal Mail Line postcards depicting games played aboard ship during the early years of this century. They were, in fact, part of the fun aboard all liners at that time and were arranged to alleviate the boredom of long passages at sea: (top left) Chalking the Pig's Eye; (top right) Slinging the Monkey; (below left) Cigarette and Necktie Race; (below right) The Bolster Bar.*

LIST OF SHIPS

(brackets indicate illustrations)